THE HERITAGE COLLECTION

LABOTSIBENI MDLULI
THE FORMIDABLE SWATI REGENT

Letitia deGraft Okyere

Illustrated by Zunaira Shabbir

Labotsibeni Mdluli: The Formidable Swati Regent

Copyright © 2022 by Letitia deGraft Okyere

Illustrator: Zunaira Shabbir

Layout designer: Nasim Malik Sarkar

Library of Congress Control Number: 2022904429

All rights reserved.

No part of this publication may be reproduced, stored in a retrieval system, a database, and/or published in any form or by any means, electronic, mechanical, photocopying, recording or otherwise, without the prior written permission of the publisher.

ISBN 978-1-956776-02-7 hardback
ISBN 978-1-956776-03-4 ebook

Published by Lion's Historian Press
https://www.lionshistorian.net/

For

Kiara Joy and Benjamin Michael

CONTENTS

Chapter 1: Early Years 1
Chapter 2: Uncle Mvelase Takes Charge 3
Chapter 3: Marriage to the King 5
Chapter 4: The Rise of Gwamile 7
Chapter 5: 1894 Convention 9
Chapter 6: Queen Mother Labotsibeni 11
Chapter 7: Queen Regent 13
Chapter 8: Plans for Labotsibeni's Removal 15
Chapter 9: Land Buy-Back 17
Chapter 10: Education Policy 19
Chapter 11: Founder of the Abantu-Batho Newspaper 21
Chapter 12: World War I Effort 23
Chapter 13: Queen Labotsibeni Transfers Power 25
Chapter 14: Queen Labotsibeni's Legacy 27
Glossary 29
Quiz 31
References 32
Acknowledgements 33
Fun Fact About the Kingdom of Eswatini (formerly, Swaziland) 34
Other Books in the Heritage Collection 35

A Brief Introduction

The Kingdom of Eswatini (or Eswatini) was known as the Kingdom of Swaziland (or Swaziland) until 2018, when the reigning monarch announced the name change in honor of King Mswati II. The citizens of the kingdom are known as the Swati. King Mswati II, referred to as one of the greatest kings of the nation, ruled from 1845 to 1868. The name Swazi was an English corruption of King Mswati II's name.

Early Years

Labotsibeni Mdluli was born around 1856 in northern Swaziland. She was given the name *labo-Tsibeni*, meaning *their Tsibeni*. At the time, her father was in a battle with Chief Tsibeni from the neighboring Bapedi state. Labotsibeni's father, Matsanjana Mdluli, belonged to King Mswati II's army.

Sadly, many from Bapedi died even though the battle was just meant to show the stronger might of the Swati. In accordance with tradition then, the Swati had to make amends for these accidental deaths by naming children after enemies. Hence, this new Mdluli child was given the name Labotsibeni in honor of Chief Tsibeni.

There is not much written about Labotsibeni's childhood. However, it is known she was full of energy, always eager to help her mother LaMabuza and neighbors with chores. Labotsibeni also enjoyed playing with her siblings at the family's homestead.

Mama LaMabuza recognized her daughter's determination and desire to improve the well-being of her community and encouraged Labotsibeni to learn family and Swati history. These lessons filled Labotsibeni with pride in her Swati heritage at an early age. The Mdluli family participated in nation-building, serving with honors in the military and as government leaders. Mama LaMabuza, on the other hand, was from the Mabuza clan, which helped to conquer land for the kingdom.

Swaziland is now known as Eswatini or officially the Kingdom of Eswatini. Eswatini is landlocked by the countries of South Africa and Mozambique in southern Africa.

Chapter 2

Uncle Mvelase Takes Charge

Sadly, Labotsibeni's father died in battle when she was young. Labotsibeni's paternal uncle, Mvelase Mdluli, Chief of the Mdluli family, became responsible for his brother's family. Mama LaMabuza moved her children to the royal estate at Ludzidzini, in central Eswatini, where Uncle Mvelase lived.

Labotsibeni developed a strong relationship with her uncle, and as a result, she became known as *Lisomi laMvelase*, the starling of Mvelase. More importantly, the move to Ludzidzini opened the door to valuable training she would need for her future. Labotsibeni did not know she would one day become Queen Mother and that it would happen at a time of great difficulty in the kingdom.

The influential Queen Mother, Tsandzile, mother of the reigning monarch King Mswati II, took Labotsibeni under her wing. Queen Mother Tsandzile gave Labotsibeni training in state affairs and diplomacy, and she gained an understanding of the kingdom's political problems. Labotsibeni received lessons in conflicts between Swati and European settlers. The settlers were mostly British or descendants of Dutch traders known as Boers. Labotsibeni also learned about protecting the role of the Swati King.

Chapter 3

Marriage to the King

When Labotsibeni came of age, the families agreed to a marriage to one of King Mswati II's sons. Labotsibeni married the reigning Swati King, Mbandzeni, known as Dlamini IV, soon after his coronation in 1874. Labotsibeni had several children with King Mbandzeni, but only three sons (Bhunu, Malunge, and Lomvazi) and daughter Tongotongo survived into adulthood. King Mbandzeni, said to be kindhearted, died in 1889.

King Mbandzeni's death left Labotsibeni with great responsibility. She had to manage the kingdom's struggle for self-government and land problems that had increased during King Mbandzeni's reign. King Mbandzeni had secured the kingdom's independence when he supported the British in a war against a neighboring group of people. However, King Mbandzeni was believed to have given away land rights to European settlers, and this threatened the Swati's right to independence and land ownership.

These land rights, known as concessions, covered activities such as farming, grazing, and mining. The Europeans would later use these concessions against the kingdom's independence, threatening an end to the Swati nation during Labotsibeni's regency.

CHAPTER 4

The Rise of Gwamile

Labotsibeni became the *Ndlovukazi*, or Queen Mother, after King Mbandzeni's death. Council elders had selected Labotsibeni's eldest son, Bhunu, to be the crown prince in 1890. The queen mother is important in Swati tradition because she controls the government as a joint ruler with the king.

Labotsibeni's rise to queen mother did not come easily. Council elders choose Swati kings after the reigning king's death, and the selection is determined by who the mother of the new king is. The new king's mother must be one of the dead king's wives, from a clan responsible for giving birth to kings, and must have only one child, a son. Labotsibeni was one of King Mbandzeni's wives, yes, but from the Mdluli clan, known for military skills, not birthing kings. Also, she had three sons.

The rules disqualified Labotsibeni on many grounds. However, the council elders believed in Labotsibeni's capacity to restore stability to the kingdom. Even though, as was common then, she had no formal education, Labotsibeni had demonstrated the strength of character and an understanding of state affairs during King Mbandzeni's reign. Labotsibeni had put her focus on securing the rights of her Swati people.

Chapter 5

1894 Convention

Labotsibeni began to participate in government matters and made decisions protecting national interests from the moment the council made her Ndlovukazi. This occurred even though she played a secondary role to the Queen Regent Tibati Nkambule. Soon, the center of Swati affairs moved from Tibati Nkambule's royal village to Labotsibeni's at Zombodze.

The British, together with the Boer state known as the South African Republic, decided to resolve land issues in southern Africa to protect settlers' interests. This led to the 1894 Convention, which put the Boers in charge of administering the kingdom. Labotsibeni led the resistance against the Convention and refused to assent to its terms. She sent a delegation to Britain to protest the transfer of the Swati nation.

The Swati delegation did not receive a positive response from Britain. However, at the later Swati Council meeting to discuss the matter, attendees rejected the transfer. Although the kingdom became a protected state of the South African Republic in 1895, Labotsibeni had sparked nationalism among the Swati people. She had increased Swati awareness of European settlers taking native land without the right to do so.

Labotsibeni endured the change and kept a respectful relationship with the new administration, but she continued to send protest letters to the governments of Britain and the Boer state.

Chapter 6

Queen Mother Labotsibeni

In February 1895, Labotsibeni's son Bhunu became king and was styled as Ngwane V. This ended Tibati's reign as queen regent and strengthened Queen Mother Labotsibeni's position.

Queen Mother Labotsibeni had to deal with the new tax imposed on the Swati by Boer administrators in 1896. Labotsibeni believed it wrong to pay taxes to an unwanted administration of foreigners and again sent protests to British and Boer representatives. Despite objections from the Swati, the Europeans implemented tax collection two years later, but it served to strengthen the Swati's resentment against European control.

Also, during this time, locals reported that Bhunu had killed one of Queen Labotsibeni's Swati advisors. Though local leaders never fully settled the facts, it led to a threat of unrest between the Swati and European settlers. The Swati would not allow the Europeans to treat Bhunu like a common criminal.

Bhunu fled to neighboring Zululand as a worried Labotsibeni negotiated with the European administrators, concerned that they planned to end the monarchy. Bhunu returned to face investigators, who found that he was not responsible for the crime. Queen Mother Labotsibeni was relieved at the outcome. With the rumor of a war between the British and Boers, Labotsibeni looked forward to Swati independence.

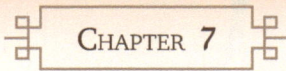

Queen Regent

Queen Mother Labotsibeni's title changed in 1899, after Bhunu's death. Council elders selected Bhunu's son, known as Nkhotfotjeni Mona, as successor. However, as Mona was only four months old, Labotsibeni became Queen Regent. Labotsibeni's priority would be to work toward independence and restoring the authority and status of the Swati monarchy.

This change in Labotsibeni's title occurred soon after the British and Boer conflict, known as the South African War. The kingdom became independent because both British and Boer administrators left, and Labotsibeni hoped to secure permanent independence after the war.

Labotsibeni preferred a British victory because she believed they were more amenable to collaboration. However, she wisely maintained a neutral position during the war to protect Swati interests. The Queen Regent successfully maintained diplomatic relationships with both British and Boer forces, keeping the Swati out of the conflict, which ended in 1902.

Plans for Labotsibeni's Removal

Labotsibeni hoped that as the British won the war, the kingdom would maintain its independent status. Unfortunately, in 1903, the British transferred the administration of the kingdom to the Boer state, renamed the Transvaal Colony.

After some three years, the kingdom was transferred to direct British control. Also, the British canceled the private income Labotsibeni received from concessions. This was a critical source of money for the monarchy. These actions added to Labotsibeni's belief that the British planned to strip the Swati of its right to self-government.

When British Administrator Coryndon arrived in the kingdom in 1907, he wrote to his Senior British Administrator complaining about Queen Regent Labotsibeni, wanting to have her removed. Coryndon argued that Labotsibeni would pass the kingship to her second son, Malunge, instead of her grandson, Crown Prince Mona.

However, Labotsibeni enjoyed the support of her people, and Coryndon underestimated the Queen Regent's determination. Coryndon forgot Labotsibeni's adopted name, Gwamile, meaning *unshakeable*. Rather than allow Coryndon to have his way, she continued her duties. She sent petitions to Britain seeking answers on the status of the kingdom. Labotsibeni remained strong in her convictions, and the threat of her removal passed.

Chapter 9

Land Buy-Back

Labotsibeni soon had another problem she had to deal with. The British decided King Mbandzeni had given land away and, in 1909, divided the kingdom. Labotsibeni bitterly complained to the British administrators, sending a delegation to Britain. She argued that Europeans had no land rights in the kingdom, and they could not separate the Swati from the land. However, the British ignored her pleas and cut up the kingdom, with one-third to the Swatis and the rest to concession owners.

Labotsibeni recognized that she could not drive the Europeans out. The only way to secure a future for her people would be to buy back the land given away to concession owners. Labotsibeni asked Swati chiefs to collect funds from each Swati male to repurchase the land from the Europeans. Labotsibeni reclaimed pieces of land in her buy-back effort.

The British tried everything to stop the campaign, even passing a law in January 1915 to vest control of land purchased in the senior British Administrator. However, Labotsibeni was eventually successful in getting the British administration to approve her buy-back program.

Labotsibeni's grandson Mona, who became known as King Sobhouza II, restarted the buy-back program in the 1940s, strengthening the Swati case for independence. The effort was so successful that by 1968, Swati rights had increased from 37% at the time of the partition to 63%.

Chapter 10

Education Policy

In her younger days, Labotsibeni believed that traditional education provided adequate preparation for children of the royal family and its advisers. As a result, she rejected western education for her son Bhunu. However, Labostibeni later understood the power of Europeans rested in having a good education, and she established the foundation for education in the kingdom. Labotsibeni decided the Swati must adapt to modern standards.

Labotsibeni convinced the British administration to assist in her educational efforts. After the war, she asked the British for a school, and in 1911, the Zombodze National School opened. Crown Prince Mona and other royal children attended school for the first time. After primary education, they went to South Africa for high school. Labotsibeni also established a Swati national fund for technical, industrial, agricultural, and other skills training.

Later, influenced by his grandmother Labotsibeni, King Sobhouza II improved Zombodze National by adding a high school so Swatis did not have to travel to South Africa.

CHAPTER 11

Founder of the Abantu-Batho Newspaper

Labotsibeni decided to collaborate with others involved in the fight against colonial oppression when the Europeans created a union in southern Africa. In 1912, a young lawyer called Pixley kaIsaka Seme and others formed the South African Native National Congress to promote unity among Africans. Labotsibeni actively supported the group, and she registered her young grandson, Crown Prince Mona, as a founding member. This group later became the African National Congress which fought to end apartheid in South Africa and secure the release of one of its leaders, Nelson Mandela, from prison.

Later in 1912, Pixley ka Seme asked Labotsibeni to help establish the Abantu-Batho (The People) weekly paper. In addition to providing funding, Labotsibeni ensured that Abantu-Batho published stories about issues important to natives in southern Africa. Labotsibeni wanted to encourage other southern Africans to fight for self-government.

The paper was published in several African languages so diverse groups could read it. The newspaper helped build international support for the Swati and other natives in southern Africa. Abantu-Batho became the voice of repressed Africans in the south of Africa.

World War I Effort

During World War I, Labotsibeni voluntarily provided funds to support the British war effort, even though she had been displeased when the British failed to acknowledge the kingdom's contribution during the South African War.

The British would use the funds to purchase a warplane for British forces. The inscription made on the plane, "By the Chief Regent, Chiefs, and people of Swaziland," ensured that the world would not forget the contribution by Africans to the British resistance. Also, Labotsibeni believed the donation would remind the British of Swati support, thus moving the British to meet its responsibilities to the Africans.

Labotsibeni became one of few African women who visibly contributed to the British war effort. The Queen Regent had informed the British Administrator that the Swati were prepared to stand with the British.

Chapter 13

Queen Labotsibeni Transfers Power

In 1921, Queen Regent Labotsibeni handed over the reins of government to her grandson, Crown Prince Mona, when he was twenty-two years old. He became known as King Sobhuza II, the longest-serving Swati monarch. At the ceremony, Queen Regent Labotsibeni remarked that since King Mbandzeni's death in 1899, "My life has been burdened with an awful responsibility." She was glad to pass national duties to a younger generation.

Labotsibeni managed Swati affairs for thirty-two years, as Queen Mother and twice as Queen Regent, during the youth of Crown Prince Bhunu and Crown Prince Mona. During these three decades, she dealt with many issues, including the Swati loss of independence, threats to the monarchy, and division of Swati land. However, she remained unshakeable and formidable, wisely addressing each problem. Though she opposed the British, she learned to adapt to changing times, collaborating with the British to secure the kingdom's future.

CHAPTER 14

Queen Labotsibeni's Legacy

Labotsibeni Mdluli died in December 1925, when she was about eighty years old. Today, women across the globe celebrate Labotsibeni's lifetime achievements. In 1975, during the Swati International Women's Day celebrations, national leaders unveiled a statue in honor of the great Queen Mother. National stamps were also issued that same year in Labotsibeni's memory. In 2019, the council of the capital city, Mbabane, erected a statue of Labotsibeni on a primary street, unveiled by the reigning monarch, His Majesty King Mswati III.

Queen Regent Labotsibeni stands tall among leaders in southern Africa, whether male or female. Labotsibeni refused to allow being a woman to hinder her fight for the Swati Kingdom, and colonial administrators agreed that Labotsibeni was a force that they could not deny. Labotsibeni lived up to her adopted name, Gwamile, the unshakeable one. A proud Swati, she remained faithful to her traditional roots and defended her country against colonial encroachment.

During King Sobhouza II's youth, Labotsibeni predicted that one day her grandson would get back the Swatis' land. In 1968, under King Sobhouza II's leadership, the British granted Independence to the kingdom, and the Queen Regent's dream came to pass.

Glossary

Swaziland — Now known as Eswatini, is one of the smallest countries in Africa and is landlocked in southern Africa.

Ndlovukazi — Meaning *Great She Elephant*, is the queen mother's title for the mother of the reigning monarch in Eswatini.

Boers — This describes descendants of Dutch, French, and other Europeans who settled on the Cape of Good Hope in southern Africa.

Queen Regent — A person appointed to govern a country because the monarch is too young or unable to govern.

The South African War — Also known as the Second Boer War, was fought by the British against two Boer states, the South African Republic, and Orange Free State. After the British victory, they became British colonies.

The South African Republic — A Boer state in southern Africa also known as ZAR. After the South African War, it became the Transvaal Colony. It is now a part of the modern-day Republic of South Africa (or South Africa).

Zululand — This was a kingdom in southern Africa, close to Eswatini, at one time ruled by the great King Shaka. It is now part of the Republic of South Africa (or South Africa).

Apartheid	This was a system of separation or discrimination based on race in the Republic of South Africa, putting black Africans at the lowest end of the social structure.
Buy-Back	This was a campaign established by Queen Labotsibeni to restore native lands to the Swati. These were lands said to have been given to European settlers through concessions.
Abantu-Batho	This weekly newspaper published in southern Africa helped Africans discuss critical issues of the time, like colonial repression and the loss of native lands to European settlers.
Nation-building	The act of bringing together a group of people with a common identity as a state or nation.

Quiz

1. What was Labotsibeni's father's name?
   (a) Malunge Mdluli
   (b) Matsanjana Mdluli
   (c) Mabuza Mdluli
   (d) Mvelase Mdluli

2. Who was the queen mother who gave Labotsibeni training she would need later to govern the Swati kingdom?
   (a) Ntombi
   (b) Lomawa
   (c) Tibati
   (d) Tsandzile

3. What percentage of Swati land was lost when the British divided up the country?
   (a) 50%
   (b) 80%
   (c) 60%
   (d) 10%

4. Who did the queen regent hand over the government to in 1921?
   (a) Sobhuza II
   (b) Ngwane V
   (c) Sobhuza I
   (d) Mswati II

Quiz Answers: BDCA

References

Mokoatsi, Thapelo. Pioneers: Swazi Queen Labotsibeni
http://www.thejournalist.org.za/spotlight/pioneers-swazi-queen-labotsibeni-2/
8/13/2021.

Mkhonza, S. (2012). Queen Labotsibeni and Abantu-Batho. In G. Christison, P. Landau, P. Limb, C. Lowe, S. Mkhonza, S. Ndlovu, et al. (Authors), *The People's Paper: A centenary history and anthology of Abantu-Batho* (pp. 128-150). Wits University Press. Johannesburg.

Kanduza, Ackson. (2001) 'You Are Tearing My Skirt': Labotsibeni Gwamile LaMdluli. In Youé C., Stapleton T. (Eds.), *Agency and Action in Colonial Africa* (pp. 83-99). Palgrave Macmillan, London.

Gillis, D. Hugh Gillis. *The Kingdom of Swaziland: Studies in Political History*. London, Greenwood Press, 1999.

Ginindza, Thoko. "Labotsibeni/Gwamile Mdluli: The Power Behind the Swazi Throne, 1875-1925." *Annals of the New York Academy of Sciences*, vol. 810, 1997, pp.135-158.

Acknowledgements

I would like to acknowledge Francis Daniels, Slbusiso Hlatshwayo, Rich Mkhondo, Slpho Khoza (Mahlatsi High School, Mupmalanga), and Joy Ndwandwe (Founding President, Indigenous Knowledge Hub of the Kingdom of Eswatini), for assistance with understanding the meaning and significance of the name, Labotsibeni.

Fun Fact About the Kingdom of Eswatini (formerly, Swaziland)

The Kingdom of Eswatini is the smallest country in Africa. It measures 6,704 suare miles and it is slightly smaller than the state of Massachusettes in the U.S.A. The Kingdom of Eswatini is bordered from north, across the west to the southeast by South Africa, and on northeast corner, by Mozambique.

Other Books in the Heritage Collection

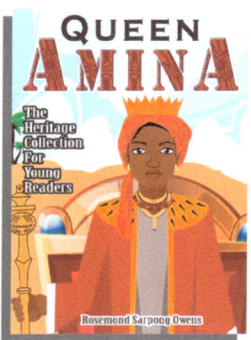 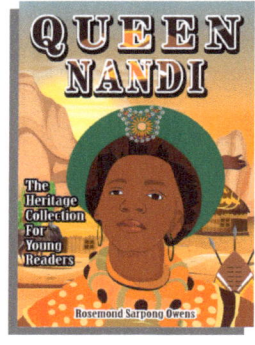  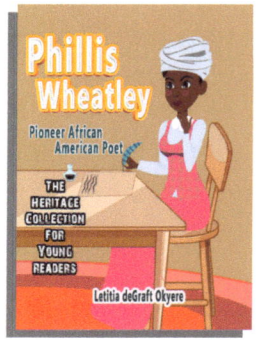

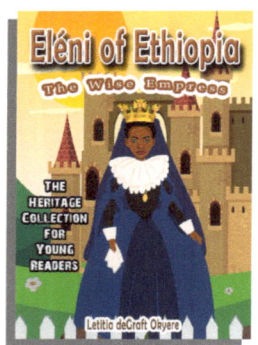 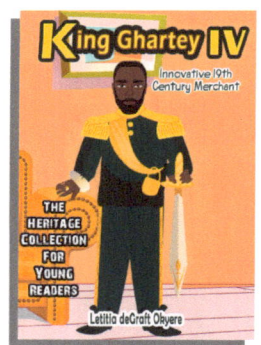 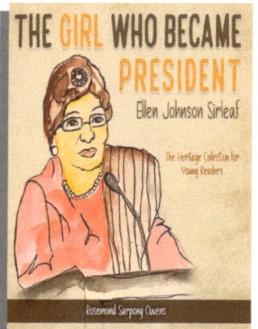 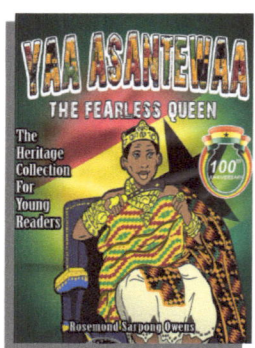

Inform • Inspire • Imagine

www.ingramcontent.com/pod-product-compliance
Lightning Source LLC
Chambersburg PA
CBHW040757240426
43673CB00014B/370